PUGH'S CREATURES GREAT AND SMALL

PUGH

For Frank Snr and Frank Jnr

*"I've got a confession to make.
I've never liked bungalows."*

"They're not the best
looking pair but you can't
fault their technique."

"We said 300 carats,
not carrots."

"Oh hello, it's you again."

WHY DINOSAURS DIED OUT...

"This is the fourth health
check you've given me today."

"You're too aggressive! Have you considered changing your diet?!"

"I've heard of homing pigeons
but this is ridiculous!"

"I think we can take it he prefers chocolate drops."

"Could we make an exception
to allow one colleague to
work from the beach?"

"Lunch is nearly ready..."

"What does that say?
478 Facebook friends invited
and only the dog turns up."

*"I said I hope the snake
isn't too underdone?..."*

"Would anybody else here like to confess that they've been eating meat?"

"Let's see what happens.
I've told it to wake us at 7."

"I understand you have a
grumble, Mattison. Do come
in and explain..."

"I'm not saying it's perfect
but it speeds up the
vaccination process."

"I'll be honest, you're not
what I was expecting either."

"The annoying thing is I hadn't stopped..."

"Without him I'd never remember my password."

"He hasn't been the same since his diversity course."

"What's the capital of
North Macedonia?"

"It's not perfect but it's quicker than Royal Mail."

"May I introduce our expert
in cattle flatulence..."

"You wanted to see me?"

"I'm going vegetarian –
I want to live longer!"

"Since he's had the dog his social life's picked up no end."

"I'm not sure the herd immunity strategy is working, Kenneth."

"I'll believe it when I see it."

"Limp past and watch his
face – it's priceless!"

"Be super-vigilant. Apparently China has a spy in our midst..."

"We were so pleased to find some affordable childcare."

"You've forgotten my birthday again this year."

"Hazel, could you bring in a
cup of tea and some plankton?"

*"I think the cat wants
to come in."*

"I'm afraid the results won't be ready until after Christmas."

"This is absurd – the dog's been upgraded to first class."

"Oh, for heaven's sake! Roll up a magazine and swat it!"

"I don't believe it! Look over there – a GP!"

"See? You're already getting
colour in your cheeks!"

"Brushing is fine but is the flossing necessary?!"

"It's a challenging mission to Beijing. Can we rely on you to avoid any honeytraps?"

"Oh look, it's the first cuckoo of spring."

"This road's always
been a rat run."

*"If you've seen a slug, darling,
pick it up and throw it into
next door's garden."*

"There was a zebra crossing there and you didn't even see it!"

"You're in luck – we've given
up meat for January."

"To be fair, he was having sushi for lunch before it became fashionable."

"Tiddles?!!"

"Have you got any proof
that you're all from the
same household?"

"That was a silly present!"

"Thank heavens decking is going out of fashion."

"He's very good at choosing the freshest fish."

"We have another complaint about the potholes."

"I don't know where he gets
the energy fron..."

"I was a town mouse but
I couldn't afford a
property in London."

"I think the egg may be past its sell-by date."

"Hang on, that's not an olive branch! It's a piece of plastic!"

ACKNOWLEDGMENTS

There are a number of people who have made this book possible: Ted Verity, my wonderful editor at The Daily Mail, and his predecessors, Geordie Grieg and Paul Dacre, who, between them, originally chose these cartoons for publication in the newspaper. Huge thanks to the amazing and unflappable Stuart Pinkney for helping to edit the cartoons and for single-handedly putting this book together; it would not have got off the ground without him. Thank you to Studio Tunnard for their inspired idea for the book title *Pugh's Creatures Great & Small*. Above all, I would like to thank my incredible wife, Anna.

ABOUT THE AUTHOR

Award-winning cartoonist, Pugh, initially studied law (which presented him with hours of doodling practice), then, after a brief stint as an art teacher, began his career as a freelance cartoonist in 1987.

In 1995, he joined *The Times* and was, for many years, their daily front-page cartoonist.

In 2010, he became the pocket cartoonist for the *Daily Mail*, where his work appears today.

As well as being involved with various projects and books, he also draws a weekly cartoon for *The Tablet*.

instagram.com/pughcartoons

ORDER PRINTS

If you'd like to buy a print of a Pugh cartoon that's appeared in the Daily Mail, please go to:

mailpictures.newsprints.co.uk/pughs-cartoon-collection